Oxford Reading Tree

Myself

FACT FINDERS

Keeping healthy

John Foster

Oxford University Press 1994

These children look healthy.
How can you keep healthy?
This book is about keeping healthy.

Contents

Healthy eating

Food gives you energy.

Food helps you to grow.

You need different foods.

Different foods keep you healthy.

Protein foods

nuts

chicken

fish

bread

meat

pasta

egg

cheese

These protein foods help you to grow.
Eat some of these foods every day.

Different foods

These foods are good for you.
You can eat lots of them.

These foods give you lots of energy.
But do not eat too much of them.

Looking after your teeth

Learn how to brush your teeth.

Brushing keeps your teeth clean.

It keeps your gums and teeth healthy.

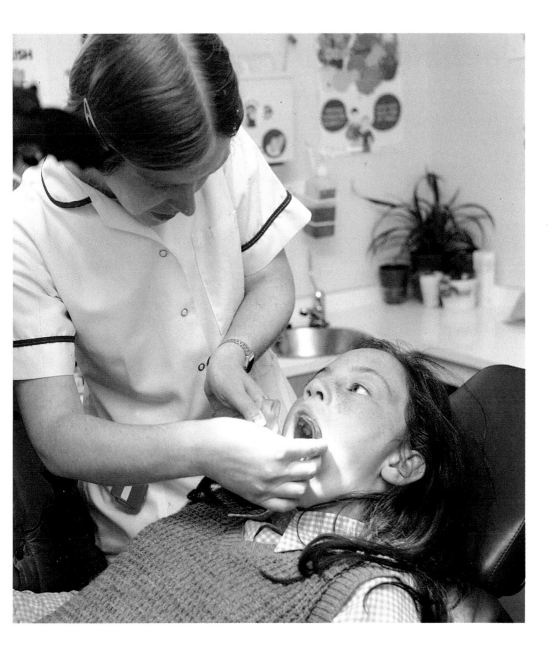

The dentist looks at your teeth to make sure they are healthy.

Keeping clean

You need to wash every day.
Soap and water keep your body clean.

Wash your hands before you eat.

Dirty hands can have germs on them.

The germs can make you ill.

Getting exercise

Exercise keeps you fit and healthy.
Exercise helps you to grow stronger.

You need some exercise every day.
There are many ways to get exercise.

Getting rest

You need rest to keep healthy.
You get rest when you sleep.

Children need a lot of sleep, because their bodies are still growing.

Index

Oxford University Press, Walton Street, Oxford OX2 6DP

© Oxford University Press
All rights reserved

First published by Oxford University Press 1994
Reprinted 1995

ISBN 0 19 916631 5
Available in packs
Myself pack (one of each title)
ISBN 0 19 916634 X
Myself class pack (six of each title)
ISBN 0 19 916635 8

Teacher's Guide ISBN 0 19 916670 6

Acknowledgements

The publisher would like to thank the following for
permission to reproduce photographs: Sally and Richard
Greenhill (pp 8, 9); John Walmsley (pp12, 13).

All other photographs by Martin Sookias

Illustrated by: Alex Brychta(p2); Daniel, Christopher, and
Julie Kennedy (children's poster p5).
Also thanks to Lou Smith.

Printed and bound in Hong Kong